Bison

By Mara Grunbaum

Children's Press®

An Imprint of Scholastic Inc.

Nature's CHILDREN™

Content Consultant
Nikki Smith
Assistant Curator, North America and Polar Frontier
Columbus Zoo and Aquarium

Library of Congress Cataloging-in-Publication Data

Names: Grunbaum, Mara, author.
Title: Bison/by Mara Grunbaum.
Description: New York, NY: Children's Press, an imprint of Scholastic Inc.,
2019. | Series: Nature's children | Includes bibliographical references and index.
Identifiers: LCCN 2018003317| ISBN 9780531192603 (library binding) |
ISBN 9780531137536 (paperback)
Subjects: LCSH: Bison—Juvenile literature.
Classification: LCC QL737.U53 G78 2019 | DDC 599.64/3—dc23
LC record available at https://lccn.loc.gov/2018003317

Design by Anna Tunick Tabachnik

Creative Direction: Judith E. Christ for Scholastic

Produced by Spooky Cheetah Press

Printed in North Mankato, MN, USA 113

SCHOLASTIC, CHILDREN'S PRESS, NATURE'S CHILDREN™, and associated logos
are trademarks and/or registered trademarks of Scholastic Inc.

1 2 3 4 5 6 7 8 9 10 R 28 27 26 25 24 23 22 21 20 19

Scholastic Inc., 557 Broadway, New York, NY 10012.

Table of Contents

Fact File..4

CHAPTER 1   **Massive Mammals**.........................6
                   Built Tough.................................8
                   Herd Mentality............................11

CHAPTER 2   **Home on the Range**....................12
                   Winter Warriors..........................15
                   Pest Control................................16
                   Friends of the Prairie...................19

CHAPTER 3   **Being a Bison**..............................20
                   Mating Season............................23
                   Big Babies...................................24
                   On the Move...............................27

CHAPTER 4   **Ancient Migration**.....................28
                   Bison vs. Buffalo.........................31
                   Beasts of Burden........................32

CHAPTER 5   **A History with Humans**..............34
                   Overhunted..................................37
                   Back from the Brink.....................38
                   Facing the Future........................41

Bison Family Tree.......................................42
Words to Know..44
Find Out More..46
Facts for Now..46
Index...47
About the Author...48

Fact File: Bison

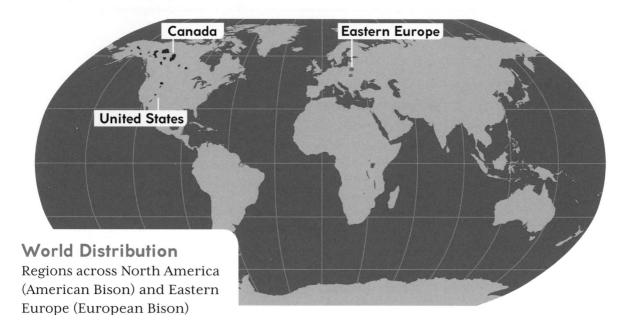

Canada

Eastern Europe

United States

World Distribution
Regions across North America (American Bison) and Eastern Europe (European Bison)

Habitat
Grasslands and meadows on the North American prairie and in Eastern Europe

Habits
Spend much of their time grazing on grasses and chewing food; travel in large herds; historically, migrated long distances to find food

Diet
Mainly grasses and sedges; also moss, lichens, leaves, and flowering plants

Distinctive Features
Massive bodies with prominent shoulder humps; feet covered with hard hooves; shaggy hair on the shoulders and long, dark mane around the neck; curved, pointy horns on both males and females

Fast Fact
The biggest bison can weigh as much as a small car.

Average Size

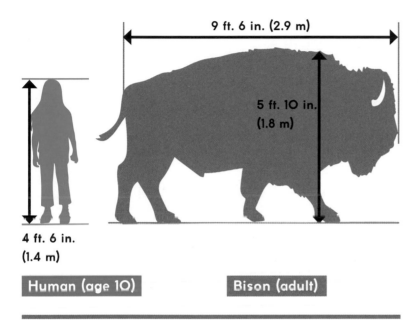

9 ft. 6 in. (2.9 m)

5 ft. 10 in. (1.8 m)

4 ft. 6 in. (1.4 m)

Human (age 10)

Bison (adult)

Classfication

CLASS
Mammalia
(mammals)

ORDER
Artiodactyla (hoofed
mammals with an even
number of toes)

FAMILY
Bovidae (antelope,
bison, buffalo, cattle,
goats, and sheep)

GENUS
Bison
(bison)

SPECIES
· *Bison bison*
  (American bison)
· *Bison bonasus*
  (European bison)

◀ Bison have poor
eyesight, but their
senses of hearing and
smell are excellent.

CHAPTER 1

Massive Mammals

The sun is rising over a hillside in Yellowstone National Park. It's quiet except for the whistling wind. Then suddenly the ground starts shaking. From the distance comes a low rumbling sound. A cloud of dust appears on the horizon. A moment later, a gigantic **herd** of animals thunders down the hill. It's a bison **stampede**!

Bison are the largest **mammals** in North America. They stand up to 6.5 feet (2 meters) tall and weigh about 2,000 pounds (907.2 kilograms). They live on the **prairie**, where they eat grasses and shrubs.

There were once more bison than people in North America. But in the 1800s, people hunted huge numbers of bison. The enormous animals almost became **extinct**.

In the 1890s, **conservationists** began to help this icon of the American West. Now about 31,000 bison live in national parks and nature **reserves**.

▶ Charging bison can reach speeds of up to 35 mph (56.3 km/h).

Tail

hangs down when the bison is relaxed and stands up straight when it's angry.

Built Tough

If you stood face-to-face with a bison, there are a few things you might notice first. One is the animal's gigantic head. It's covered in dark, shaggy hair, which grows into a beard beneath the bison's chin. This keeps the bison's face warm in the cold.

Next are the bison's extremely large neck muscles. They form a tall hump behind the bison's head. The muscles in the hump enable the bison to swing its big head back and forth. In winter, it uses its head like a bulldozer to move snow out of its way.

Thick, light brown hair covers a bison's neck, shoulders, and front legs. Shorter hair grows on its backside. In winter, a thick coat grows over the bison's whole body to keep it warm.

Male bison are larger and heavier than females. Both have short, pointy horns. Tough hooves cover the bison's toes. They support the massive animal's weight when it walks and runs.

Hump
is made of muscles that move the bison's giant head.

Horns
defend against predators and other bison.

Shaggy Hair
helps keep the bison warm.

Hooves
protect the bison's feet and allow it to run fast.

Fast Fact
Bison "talk" to one
another with loud
grunts and snorts.

Herd Mentality

Bison may not look too friendly, but they're actually
very **social** animals. Most bison travel in big groups
called herds. These groups can contain from 20 to 1,000
animals, depending on the time of year.

Female bison and their young make up the biggest herds.
They all travel together in search of food. Some males may
join to form smaller herds. Other males spend most of their
time in pairs or alone. In summer, the male and female
herds gather together to **mate**.

Living in a herd has advantages. Bison can work as a team
to scare off **predators** such as wolves and grizzly bears.
When one of these hunters approaches, the herd may turn
and charge straight at it. Even fierce predators find this
frightening. They scamper off to find an easier meal.

◀ A herd of
bison faces down
a gray wolf
in Yellowstone
National Park.

CHAPTER 2

Home on the Range

Bison are so big, it's hard to believe they're **herbivores**. The gigantic animals spend 9 to 11 hours a day feeding on prairie grass.

Each meal is a complicated process. That's because bison are **ruminants**. Their stomachs have four chambers, and food passes through each one. The bison barely chews before swallowing the first time. The food enters the first chamber of the stomach, where it begins to break down. Later, the food moves into the second stomach chamber. From there it's coughed back into the bison's mouth. The bison chews this **cud** to break it down further. Then it swallows it again. The last two stomach chambers finish digesting the food.

Bison don't stay in the same place for long. If they did, they'd quickly eat all the available food. Bison move about 2 miles (3.2 kilometers) every day to graze on different parts of the prairie.

▶ Bison use their muscular tongues to rip up mouthfuls of grass.

Winter Warriors

In spring and summer, bison explore northern areas. They wander up mountains to feed and raise their young. In autumn, they move south and down into valleys.

Winters on the prairie are long, cold, and windy. Luckily, bison have **adaptations** that help them survive. As winter approaches, they grow thick hair all over their bodies. This extra layer keeps them comfortable in temperatures as low as -49°F (-45°C). That's about as cold as the North Pole!

Grass becomes harder to find in winter. When that happens, bison also eat **lichens** and moss. This food is often buried under deep snow. The bison use their heads to dig out the frozen meals.

When spring arrives, bison shed their shaggy coats. They rub on trees to help loosen the hair. They won't need it until the next winter. But the warm season brings its own share of troubles.

◀ A strong sense of smell helps bison find food in the snow.

15

Pest Control

In warmer weather, prairie insects buzz with activity. Bison are often attacked by mosquitoes and biting flies. The bison try to use their tails as flyswatters. But the tails are too short to reach most of their bodies. Many insects bite the bison, leaving itchy welts on their skin.

To soothe the itching, bison roll in the dirt. This behavior is called **wallowing**. A bison lies on its side and rocks back and forth to coat its skin in dust. But it can't roll from one side onto the other. Its huge shoulder hump gets in the way. Instead, it stands up, then lies back down the other way.

Bison often use the same spots to wallow over and over. After a while, their giant bodies carve craters in the dirt. There are parts of the prairie where bison haven't lived for centuries. But the spots where they once wallowed are still there.

▶ Bison wallow most in early afternoon, when insects are most active.

Grizzly Bear

▶ This huge mammal hunts small or weak bison, not healthy adults.

Magpie

▶ Magpies help bison by picking insects out of their coats.

Coyote

▶ Dead bison make a convenient meal for coyotes.

Prairie Dog

Prairie dogs can find more plants in shortened grass that bison have grazed.

Friends of the Prairie

Bison are an important part of the prairie **ecosystem**. They help keep hundreds of other species alive. Predators such as bears, wolves, and mountain lions can hunt young or sick bison. Magpies perch on top of bison and eat insects from their coats. Other birds follow in the bisons' big, heavy footsteps. These birds eat bugs that the bison kick up.

Bison also transform the landscape in ways that help other species. By eating old, dry grass, they make it harder for fires to spread. Trimming the grass also makes it easier for prairie dogs to find food. When it rains, the bisons' wallowing spots fill with water. They become miniature ponds, where many smaller plants and animals can live.

Bison even help the ecosystem after they die. **Scavengers** such as coyotes feed on the bisons' huge bodies. As the bison **decompose**, they nourish the soil, allowing new prairie grasses to grow.

◀ Bison provide food—in a variety of forms—for many different animals on the prairie.

CHAPTER 3

Being a Bison

Bison in the wild can live for up to 15 years. For much of that time, they **migrate** in herds.

Herds are always moving to find food and water. Unlike many animals, bison don't migrate along a set path. Instead, they wander in different directions. They might explore an unknown area or follow an interesting smell. The older, more experienced bison lead the way. Their curiosity helps them discover new sources of food.

In July and August, bison form larger herds than usual. Hundreds of them meet up in the same spots on the prairie. Bison may travel as far as 150 mi. (241.4 km) to reach these gatherings, called ruts. It's their longest journey, but also their most important. It's the only chance for males and females to come together to mate.

▶ Yellowstone National Park is home to the largest wild bison herd.

Mating Season

Female bison, called cows, are ready to mate when they're
two years old. Male bison, or bulls, usually wait longer.
That's because they have to compete over females during
the rut. They need to grow big and strong enough to fight.
At about seven years old, a male is finally up to the
challenge. He approaches a group of females guarded by
another bull. The two males grunt and roar at each other.
They kick the dirt and wallow on the ground. They're each
trying to prove that they're more powerful. They want to
scare their opponent into giving up.

The weaker male will often back off after this display.
If he doesn't, the two bulls fight. They butt heads and
use their horns to wrestle. They kick up a storm of dust.
These battles are fierce. Both bison may be wounded. The
winner will father the next group of calves in the herd.

◄ A bison's skull is
extra thick around the
forehead to protect its
brain when it fights.

Big Babies

Spring is an exciting time on the prairie. In late April and early May, baby bison, called calves, are born. Each cow can have one baby each year. She's pregnant for just over nine months. When it's time to give birth, she finds a quiet spot away from the herd.

A newborn bison calf weighs about 50 lb. (22.7 kg). It's redder than its parents and a little wobbly on its feet. But within three hours, it learns to run. At first, the calf drinks its mother's milk. After two weeks, it also starts eating grass. In two months, the calf starts growing its hump and horns. Soon after that, it begins to turn dark brown.

Bison mothers keep a close eye on their offspring. A small calf is vulnerable to predators if it becomes separated from the herd. After a year, the young bison stops **nursing**. But it stays with its mother's herd until it's at least three years old.

▶ Calves are often referred to as "red dogs" because of the color of their coats.

On the Move

As a baby bison grows up, it travels with its mother. It must be ready for anything! The herd's migrations can take them up and down mountains. They must cross rivers and streams.

If a river crossing is shallow enough, bison simply walk across it. If the water is deeper, they swim. Most bison are strong swimmers. They can cross rivers more than half a mile (0.8 km) wide. But baby bison have to be careful. In a rushing river, a strong current can sweep them away. They watch the rest of the herd carefully. They try to cross the same way the adults do.

At night, the herd typically rests. All the adult bison take turns acting as lookouts while the rest of the herd lies down to sleep. This keeps the animals safe from predators as they rest up for their next day of travel.

◄ A young bison follows its mother across a river in Yellowstone.

CHAPTER 4

Ancient Migration

About 150,000 years ago, Earth looked very different from the way it looks today. Ice covered many of the planet's northern areas. A bridge of land connected the places we now call Alaska and Russia. Scientists think that's when bison first came to North America. Their **ancestors** lived in Asia and Europe. Some herds migrated over the land bridge and spread across the new continent.

Scientists have found **fossils** of ancient bison in Alaska and northern Canada. These animals were about the same size as modern bison but had longer horns. They were the ancestors of bison today.

American bison still have relatives in eastern Europe. European bison live in forests there. These animals look similar to American bison, but they're smaller and have less shaggy hair. Like American bison, they were once hunted until they nearly became extinct.

▶ **These Native American bison carvings are 2,000 years old.**

Bison vs. Buffalo

Many people call American bison "buffalo." But scientists don't usually use this name. That's because there are other mammals called buffalo. These animals look somewhat similar to bison, but they are different.

African buffalo live in central and southern Africa. They're only about 4.6 ft. (1.4 m) tall. Another **species**, the water buffalo, comes from Asia. Water buffalo live in forests and swamps. Both types of buffalo have longer horns than bison have. Buffalo heads and necks are much smaller. They don't have the large shoulder humps that bison do.

European explorers first saw American bison in the 1600s. They thought the animals looked like big, shaggy cows. They called the bison *boeuf*, which means "beef" in French. Historians think this became the name buffalo. But scientists now know that bison aren't closely related to buffalo in Africa and Asia. They're more similar to cattle and yaks. To avoid confusion, scientists use only the name bison.

◀ African buffalo have longer horns, bigger ears, and less shaggy hair than bison do.

31

Beasts of Burden

American bison live only in North America. But they belong to a family of **bovids** that stretches all across the globe. Many members of this family have been **domesticated**. People have raised them for thousands of years. They've trained the animals to pull farm equipment and carry heavy loads.

The most common domesticated species is cattle. About 1 billion cattle live on farms and ranches around the world. They are raised for their meat, milk, and leather. Water buffalo also live with humans. They were first domesticated in Asia. But people have brought them to Europe, Africa, and the Americas. Yaks have been domesticated in the mountains of Asia. They help people carry things over steep and rocky land.

Many bison are kept on ranches in North America. In the United States, 7.5 million pounds of their meat is sold each year. But bison are not considered domesticated. They still have many wild habits. They can be dangerous to humans and need to be handled with care.

▶ People in Tibet use bovids to carry gear up and down Mount Everest.

CHAPTER 5

A History with Humans

Native Americans in the Great Plains

region once depended on bison to survive. They were hunting the massive mammals more than 10,000 years ago. Back then, hunters used spears or bows and arrows to kill bison. Sometimes they tricked a group of animals into charging off a cliff.

Plains Indians ate bison meat and carved tools from the animals' bones. Bison hair was used to make warm blankets. The skin was turned into leather for clothes. People even used bison stomachs as cooking pots.

In the 1700s, Europeans brought horses and guns to North America. Plains Indians started using both of these to hunt. On horseback, they could follow migrating bison. They moved in groups around the prairie and hunted bison all year long.

▶ Horses made hunting bison easier—but it was still dangerous work.

Overhunted

In the early 1800s, about 60 million bison lived in North America. Travelers on the prairie could see herds that stretched for miles. But that changed over the next century. As the newly formed United States expanded, the bison population shrank.

In the 1860s, American companies built railroads across the Great Plains. Passengers shot bison from the train for fun. Famous hunters like "Buffalo Bill" Cody killed thousands of bison. They sold the meat to railroad workers and new settlers in the West.

As white settlers moved westward, they fought Plains Indians over the land. The U.S. government knew the Plains Indians relied on bison. To gain an advantage, the government started killing the animals. In the 1870s, soldiers and hunters shot up to 4 million bison a year. Many Plains Indians starved as a result. Wolves and other animals that depended on bison also suffered. By 1890, fewer than 1,000 bison were left.

◀ People shooting from trains could kill huge numbers of bison.

Back from the Brink

At the end of the 1800s, bison had been hunted nearly to extinction. Conservationists began fighting to protect those that were left. In 1893, Canada passed laws against hunting bison. The United States did the same in 1894.

One of the last wild bison herds lived in Yellowstone National Park. This was a protected area, but **poachers** were still hunting the animals. By 1902, only two dozen bison were left. In one of the country's first efforts to save a wild species from extinction, park managers bought 21 bison from ranchers. They raised the animals in a protected spot and, eventually, introduced them into Yellowstone's wild herd. Over the next few decades, the population grew.

Now Yellowstone is home to about 5,000 bison. It's the largest wild bison herd left on Earth. Many smaller herds live in other parks and wildlife reserves. They number about 26,000 animals in all.

▶ There are more than 1,000 bison in Custer State Park, South Dakota.

Facing the Future

Bison no longer face extinction. But our relationship with the animals is still complex. Inside reserves like Yellowstone, bison are protected. But state officials may capture or kill the animals if they wander onto private land. That's because bison can carry a disease that sickens cattle. Cattle ranchers want to keep the bison population under control.

Many people also want to help bison. Millions of tourists admire them in national parks every year. These visitors feel a special connection to the big, odd-looking animals.

In 2016, U.S. lawmakers made the bison an official symbol. They declared it the national mammal of the United States. They did this to honor the bison's role in American history. They wanted to celebrate that bison had been saved from dying out. Like many others, they hope that this icon of the American West will roam the prairie for centuries to come.

◀ Drivers in Yellowstone often have to stop for bison!

Bison Family Tree

Bison belong to a group of mammals called ruminants. All of the animals in this group are herbivores that chew their cud. They have a common ancestor that lived about 40 million years ago. This diagram shows how bison are related to other ruminants, such as cattle, antelopes, and deer. The closer together two animals are on the tree, the more similar they are.

Sheep
stocky ruminants with woolly hair and often curly horns

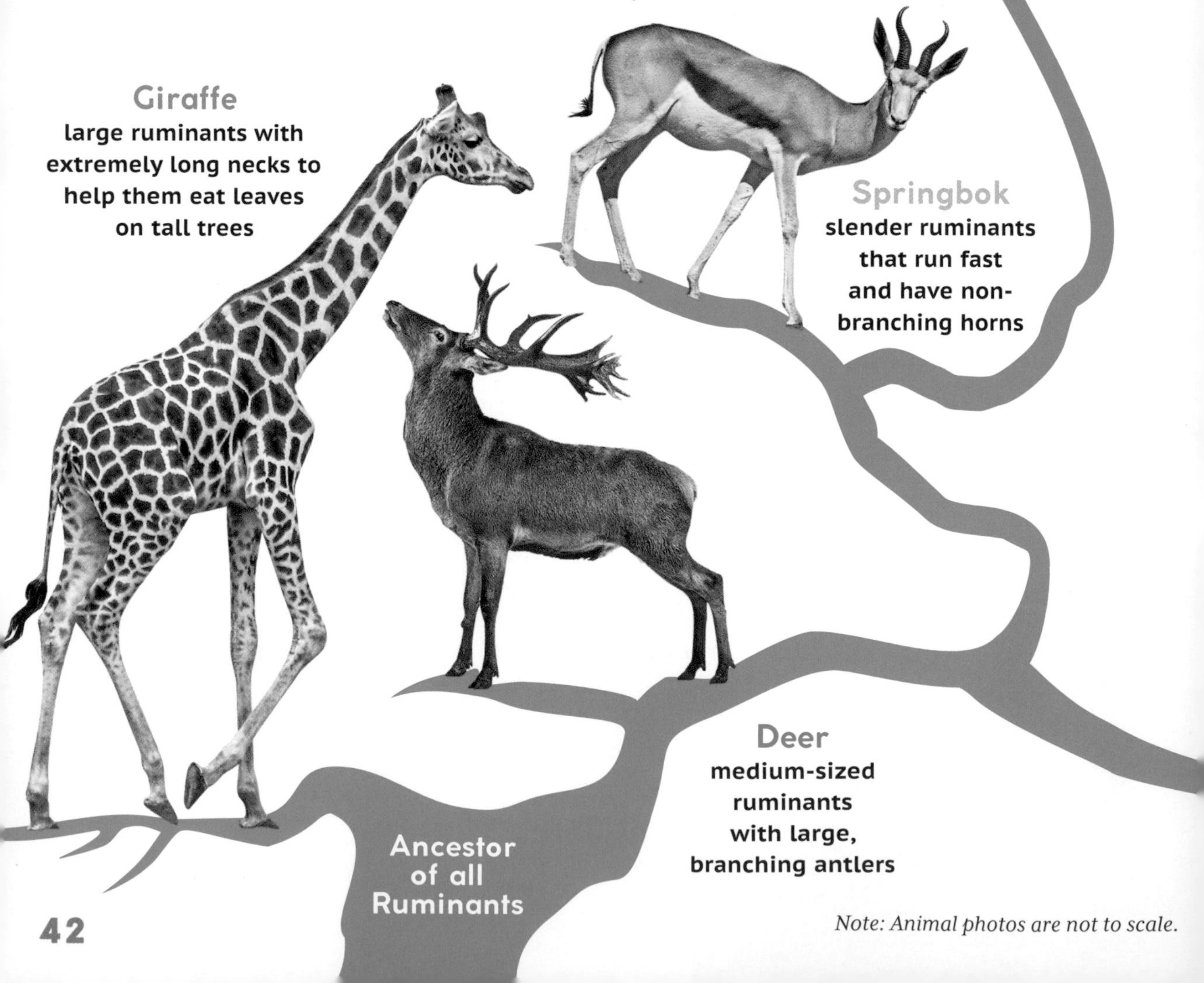

Giraffe
large ruminants with extremely long necks to help them eat leaves on tall trees

Springbok
slender ruminants that run fast and have non-branching horns

Deer
medium-sized ruminants with large, branching antlers

Ancestor of all Ruminants

Note: Animal photos are not to scale.

Yak
large, shaggy-haired ruminants with humped shoulders and long horns

Cow
large ruminants that have been domesticated for milk, meat, and leather

Bison
large ruminants with huge heads, shaggy manes, humped shoulders, and short horns

Water Buffalo
large, water-loving ruminants with extremely long, curved horns

Words to Know

A .... **adaptations** *(ad-ap-TAY-shuns)* changes a living thing goes through so it fits in better within its environment

ancestors *(ANN-sess-turs)* family members who lived long ago

B .... **bovids** *(BOW-vidz)* members of a family of ruminants with hollow horns that don't branch

C .... **conservationists** *(kahn-sur-VAY-shun-ists)* people who protect valuable things, especially forests, wildlife, or natural resources

cud *(KUD)* food from the stomach that an animal brings back up into its mouth to chew again

D .... **decompose** *(dee-kuhm-POZE)* to break down slowly because of natural processes

domesticated *(duh-MESS-tih-kay-ted)* tamed in order to live with or be used by people

E .... **ecosystem** *(EE-koh-sis-tuhm)* all the living things in a place and their relation to their environment

extinct *(ik-STINCKT)* no longer found alive

F .... **fossils** *(FAH-suhls)* bones, shells, or other traces of an animal or plant from millions of years ago, preserved as rock

H .... **herbivores** *(HUR-buh-vorz)* animals that eat only plants

herd *(HURD)* a large group of animals

L .... **lichens** *(LIE-kenz)* plantlike living things that grow on rocks and trees

M .... **mammals** *(MAM-uhlz)* warm-blooded animals that have hair or fur and usually give birth to live babies; female mammals produce milk to feed their young

mate *(MAYT)* to join together for breeding

migrate *(MYE-grate)* to move to another area or climate at a particular time of year

N **nursing** *(NURS-ing)* drinking milk from a breast

P **poachers** *(POHCH-uhrz)* people who hunt or fish illegally on someone else's property

prairie *(PREH-ree)* a wide, flat area of land where grasses and shrubs grow, but no trees

predators *(PRED-uh-tuhrs)* animals that live by hunting other animals for food

R **reserves** *(ri-ZURVZ)* protected places where hunting is not allowed and where animals can live and breed safely

ruminants *(ROO-muh-nints)* mammals that have more than one stomach and bring their food back up after swallowing to chew it again

S **scavengers** *(SKAV-uhn-jerz)* animals that eat dead and decaying material

social *(SO-shuhl)* tending to spend time together in groups

species *(SPEE-sheez)* one of the groups into which animals and plants are divided; members of the same species can mate and have offspring

stampede *(stam-PEED)* to make a sudden, wild rush in one direction, usually out of fear

W **wallowing** *(WAH-loh-ing)* rolling around in mud, dirt, or water

Find Out More

BOOKS

- Graubart, Norman D. *Bison in American History*. New York: Rosen Publishing, 2015.
- Omoth, Tyler. *American Bison*. Mendota Heights, Minn.: North Star Editions, 2016.
- Waters, Kate. *Where the Buffalo Roam: Bison in America*. New York: Penguin Young Readers, 2017.

WEB PAGES

- www.nps.gov/yell/learn/nature/bison.htm

  The Web site of Yellowstone National Park provides information about bisons' behavior, adaptations, and history, as well as the current status of the bison population there.

- www.nature.org/ourinitiatives/regions/northamerica/unitedstates/missouri/the-bison-are-coming.xml

  The Nature Conservancy Web site details an effort to reintroduce bison to a prairie habitat in Missouri.

- www.pbs.org/wnet/nature/group/mammals/american-bison/

  See clips and information from several PBS *Nature* episodes about bison.

Facts for Now

Visit this Scholastic Web site for more information on bison:
www.factsfornow.scholastic.com Enter the keyword **Bison**

Index

A

adaptations...................................15

ancestors 28, *29*

B

bovids.............................. 32, *33*

buffalo.............................. *30*, 31, 32

C

calves............*5*, 23, 24, 25, *26*, 27, *35*

cattle 31, 32, 41

Cody, "Buffalo Bill" 37

communication 11

conservation...................... 6, 38, *39*

cud..................................12

D

diet...........................6, 12, *13*, 15, 19

distribution 28, 31, 32

domestication............................ 32

E

European bison 28

extinction...................... 6, 28, 38, 41

F

female bison 8, 11, 20, 23, 24, *25*

fighting.................................. *22*, 23

G

grazing 12, *13*

H

habitat................... 6, 12, *14*, 15, 19, 27, 34, 35, *36*, 37

hair 8, *9*, 15, 28, *30*

herbivores 12

herds........6, *7*, *10*, 11, 20, *21*, 27, 38, *39*

hooves 8, *9*

horns............... 8, *9*, 23, 24, 28, *30*, 31

humps 8, *9*, 16, 24, 31

J

jumping...................................15

L

lifespan 20

M

male bison 8, 11, 20, *22*, 23

mating............................... 11, 20, 23

migration 20, 27, 28

N

Native Americans 34, *35*, 37

nursing 24

Index (continued)

P

population...............................6, 38

predators.............*10*, 11, *18*, 19, 24, 27

R

relatives................... 28, *30*, 31, 32, *33*

reserves....................................6, 38, 41

rock carvings *29*

ruminants....................................12

ruts 20, 23

S

senses....................................... 5, 15

size.................................. 4, *5*, 6, 24

species..........................*30*, 31, 32, *33*

speed...6, 7

stampedes 6, 7

swimming............................. *26*, 27

T

threats............ *10*, 11, 16, *18*, 19, 24, 27, 34, 35, *36*, 37, 38, *40*, 41

W

wallowing 16, *17*, 19

water buffalo 31, 32

Y

yaks 31, 32

About the Author

Mara Grunbaum is a science writer who loves to learn about strange and fascinating animals. She has admired bison ever since a herd of them towered over her car in Yellowstone National Park. Mara lives in Seattle, Washington.